Animals with Jobs

Rescue Dogs

Judith Janda Presnall

KIDHAVEN PRESS™

THOMSON

GALE

San Diego • Detroit • New York • San Francisco • Cleveland
New Haven, Conn. • Waterville, Maine • London • Munich

Cover photo: A German shepherd sits among rescue workers after the 1985 earthquake in Mexico City.

To all search-and-rescue teams
who dedicate many hours to finding people who are lost.

For more information, contact
KidHaven Press
27500 Drake Rd.
Farmington Hills, MI 48331-3535
Or you can visit our Internet site at http://www.gale.com

LIBRARY OF CONGRESS CATALOGING-IN-PUBLICATION DATA

Presnall, Judith Janda.
  Rescue dogs / by Judith Janda Presnall.
    v. cm.—(Animals with jobs)
Summary: Examines the job of rescue dogs to include: selection; preferred characteristics and breeds; training and abilities; rescue environments; partnerships with handlers; and support organizations.
Includes bibliographical references (p.   ).
  ISBN 0-7377-1361-5 (hardback : alk. paper)
1. Rescue dogs—Juvenile literature. [1. Rescue dogs. 2. Rescue work.]
  I. Title. II. Series.
  SF428.66 .P74 2003
  636.7'0886—dc21
                                                          2002007605

Printed in the United States of America

Contents

The Job of Rescue Dogs

The primary job of rescue dogs is to help save lives. Their most valuable service is the ability to sniff out missing people. After local or national disasters, the dogs help locate people buried under the debris of **earthquakes**, train wrecks, plane crashes, or collapsed buildings. They also find people covered by **avalanches** and victims drowned in floods or boating accidents.

The trained dogs work with human partners called handlers. These handlers include citizen volunteers as well as firefighters and police officers. Handlers choose canine partners that display special traits needed in the important job of finding people.

Characteristics

All rescue dogs share certain physical and mental characteristics. They are smart and obedient. They are willing to work and they want to please their handlers. Rescue dogs

In its search for buried survivors, a rescue dog sniffs through wreckage left by the World Trade Center attack.

get along well with other dogs and with people. They must be bold, strong, and not frightened by all the commotion at a disaster site. Many different breeds possess these traits that make them suitable for search-and-rescue work.

One example is the bloodhound, known for its strong scenting powers. Bloodhounds are used for wilderness searches both in England and in the United States.

Other large, hardy dogs, such as German shepherds, Labrador retrievers, and Newfoundlands, work well in rugged country searches. Their long legs and strong bodies allow them to work tirelessly under demanding conditions.

New York rescue workers survey the rubble at the World Trade Center site with their rescue dog.

Scent Rescues and Trail Rescues of People

Most rescue dogs specialize in air scenting or trailing. In air scenting, the dog sniffs the air to pick up human scents of both living and dead people. Air-scenting dogs are able to do their job without needing to sniff something that belongs to the lost person. Neither weather nor the passage of time affect their rescue efforts. An air-scenting dog usually works with its nose elevated, sniffing the air as the wind blows. In good terrain and in favorable weather conditions, these dogs can detect a human scent from a distance of about one-quarter mile.

Unlike air-scenting dogs, trailing dogs keep their noses to the ground. Giving trail dogs an article to smell is like showing a person a photograph.

In order to pick up the scent, these dogs first sniff an article of clothing that belonged to the lost person. The clothing has the person's skin cells on it. People are constantly shedding these cells. The cells leave a sort of invisible bread-crumb trail that is very obvious to a dog. Heavier than air, these cells fall to the ground and onto bushes. This helps the dog find the lost person.

Brad Phillips, a dog handler, once searched for a woman who had become separated from her husband during a hike through Yosemite National Park. When the search dog teams arrived, the dogs sniffed the woman's jacket. The scent from the jacket helped the dogs determine the direction in which the woman had traveled. They found her about a mile off one of the main trails—scared and cold, and relieved to be found.

Snow Rescues

Some large dogs, such as the Saint Bernard, German shepherd, and Newfoundland, use their powerful sense of smell to search for people in the snow. They rescue people lost in blizzards and avalanches. Saint Bernard dogs have been used to find buried snow victims for more than three hundred years. A Saint Bernard can locate a person buried in snow as deep as seven feet.

As early as the 1700s, Saint Bernards worked in the Swiss Alps finding snowbound travelers. In Switzerland, these hefty two-hundred-pound dogs work in teams of two. When they find the scent of a victim, they dig down toward the person. One dog lies next to the victim to keep him or her warm. The second dog runs to alert the handler, who may be farther behind. Not all snow rescues, however, are done by Saint Bernards.

German shepherds began doing snow rescues in the United States starting in the 1960s. A recent example of a successful snow rescue occurred on Mountain High, a ski area in Wrightwood, California. At this ski slope, a white German shepherd named Sequoia, owned by ski patrol canine coordinator Rick Strasser, helps skiers in trouble. In February 2000, a four-year-old boy skied away from his mother and disappeared into a five-foot hole. Noisy snowmaking machines drowned out his cries for help. Sequoia and his handler followed ski tracks into the woods. Soon Sequoia barked, telling his handler that he had found the lost boy. Whether in frozen snow or bodies of water, rescue dogs have the same goal—to save lives.

Saint Bernards are excellent for snow rescues because of their strong sense of smell.

Water Rescues

Besides land search and rescue work, Newfoundlands have natural physical traits that equip them for water rescues. Their webbed toes help them swim. Their glossy, black double coats of fur—thick, soft undercoat and a long, coarse, and oily outercoat—protect them from icy waters. The strong, 150-pound Newfoundland dogs rescue people in danger of drowning following a shipwreck or other sea accident. Swimming through waves, Newfoundlands carry lifelines to the ship or to the

Newfoundlands are trained to grab victims in the water and swim to shore.

shore in storms when ships are in danger of sinking. They also carry people to shore one at a time, with a passenger clutching to the Newfoundland's long hair. Or, the dog will use its mouth to grab a panicked victim's arm or life vest and pull the person to safety. The powerful dogs even pull small boats to shore.

The Search for Survivors

Other dog breeds receive special training that qualifies them to work at disaster sites. When large disasters happen, many teams of handlers and dogs are necessary. They help rescue victims from buildings that collapse as a result of earthquakes, tornadoes, or mudslides.

An estimated 350 specialty dogs were **deployed** to the World Trade Center in New York City after the September 11, 2001, terrorist attack. They tunneled through empty spaces and teetered on unstable steel and cement rubble trying to pick up the slightest scent of a human, dead or alive.

In any disaster, the first crew of dogs sent out with their handlers usually searches for survivors. "If people are going to be found alive, the dogs are the ones to find them,"[1] says Barry Kellogg, who supervised the Veterinary Medical Assistance Team in New York City.

A search-and-rescue team poses with its dogs after the World Trade Center attack.

After a week of searching, the goal of rescue operations changes from finding living people to recovering dead bodies.

Recovery of Bodies

In earthquakes and other disasters, many people often do not survive. (About twenty-eight hundred people perished in the grim September 11 catastrophe.) The dogs search to find the bodies.

Dogs trained to find bodies are called cadaver dogs. (Cadaver is another word for a dead body.) They are trained to recognize the scent of a dead body. Cadaver dogs must remain calm amid the noise of earth-moving equipment.

Rescue dog Gus and his trainer search through the wreckage from a collapsed corner of the Pentagon.

Before any dogs are allowed into the rubble, structural engineers investigate the area to determine if it can be explored safely. Then rescue specialists move in with their dogs. Cadaver dogs use various signals—depending on how they were trained—to let their handlers know when they have found a body. Some whine, some bark, some back away, some shiver, and some lie down.

Rescue dogs love to work because after a rescue they receive praise, hugs, and get to play tugging games with the handler. Working and getting playtime as a reward is exciting for dogs. But training for the work is a continuous and demanding process.

Chapter Two

Training

M ost search-and-rescue dogs and their handlers undergo about two years of training. During that time, a dog learns a variety of tasks. Some of these include obedience, air scenting, trailing, **agility** exercises, finding dead bodies, water rescues, and snow rescues. The ideal age for training a dog is between two months and ten months.

Puppy Training

Rescue dogs are earmarked for training from puppyhood. Besides an even temperament and strong body, handlers test puppies at retrieving a ball (for willingness to please), and their response to noises such as a ringing alarm clock (for tolerance to noise) and a stomping foot (for lack of fear).

Cuddling and playing with a puppy strengthens the bond and creates trust between the dog and its handler.

At age ten to twelve weeks, puppies learn obedience commands such as "sit," "come," "stay," and "heel." Dogs need to learn these voice commands because they often take the lead, working ahead of their handlers. For example, "wait" tells the dog to wait for its handler to catch up.

Training to Air Scent

Around the age of six months, some handlers begin teaching the dog to use their scenting abilities to air scent. First, the handler hides. The dog sniffs the air to distinguish its handler's distinct odor, and then finds the handler. After that, the handler hides with another person, and the dog

Puppies, such as this retriever, are taught to fetch thrown objects as part of their early testing and training.

finds both of them. Next, only the other person hides. Each time the dog locates someone, it is rewarded with a special treat, lavish praise, or a playful game.

Dan Comden, a search-and-rescue dog trainer and handler in Seattle, Washington, explains:

> We begin with small areas and try to work with favorable wind conditions to maximize the dog's chances for success. Longer and larger search problems are gradually introduced. If a team is having a difficult time, they're encouraged to take a step or two back in their training [exercise] to bolster the dog's confidence.[2]

Training to Trail

Some dogs do better if they can sniff an article of clothing that carries the scent of the lost person. The article must have been worn recently, and cannot have been handled by others. The dogs usually work in a harness and leash. They begin on a short trail where they can easily find someone. As training progresses, the trails become longer and the search more difficult.

To cover rough ground on searches, dogs must have agility training. They must learn to walk over debris, climb wet, slippery surfaces, and jump walls. The obstacles used for training include slides, barrels, ladders, hanging tires, planks, and logs. These obstacles resemble conditions that a dog might encounter at a disaster site. Climbing ladders and jumping through tires are the most strenuous drills for the handler/dog team.

A rescue worker rewards a dog with praise for doing a good job. Rewards make rescue dogs eager to keep working.

Cadaver Training

Not all rescues are successful in finding live victims. Sometimes too much time has passed—a week for example—for a person to survive. In this case, dogs must search for dead bodies. The dogs are not trained to find the bodies, but to find the scent of a **corpse**. During training some handlers will use body parts of human cadavers or a **placenta** donated to science.

Another object handlers use is called a pseudo corpse. This is a chemical made that smells like decomposed flesh. The handler opens a vial, gives the dog a whiff, and commands it to "find."

Water Training

Another area where dogs find cadavers is in the water. Water training for dogs is provided in three areas. Dogs search from a boat, from the shore, or while swimming. The dog must learn to detect human scent coming from under the water, to become accustomed to riding in a variety of small boats, and to search while swimming, if it becomes necessary.

First, a diver wearing scuba gear enters the water out of sight of the dog. The diver lingers a few feet below the surface. When the dog is downwind of the diver's scent, it will bark, whine, or paw the water. If the dog is in a boat, it may scratch at the bottom of the boat, bite the water, or even jump overboard.

If the dog is onshore, it may swim toward the direction of the scent. The handler then signals the diver to surface, and they both reward the dog for the find.

Newfoundlands train to assist lifeguards in deep-water rescues.

If a diver is not available for training, recently worn clothing is weighted and placed below the water surface. Dogs have found victims in water as deep as eighty feet.

Snow-Avalanche Training

As in water searches, there is little chance of finding victims alive after an avalanche. Dogs must find buried victims quickly before they **suffocate** or freeze to death. It takes a year of constant practice before a dog becomes certified to perform snow rescues.

To train a dog for snow avalanche rescues, the trainer first buries a bundle of clothing. After the dog has successfully found the clothing several times, it will then be trained to find a buried human. Before the dog can be certified as fully trained, it must find live victims over and over again. Serving as a volunteer victim is dangerous, and the feat is performed only under controlled circumstances. The volunteer must have steady nerves and have confidence in the dogs and their handlers.

A practice slope is chosen, and the volunteer lies buried in a pit about three to six feet deep. A space is hollowed out at the head to create a pocket of air. In case of emergency, the victim has a radio to communicate with the people above ground. All markings are erased on the snow above the pit. The dog and handler are brought to the area and given ten to fifteen minutes to find the victim.

An Avalanche Rescue

One example of an avalanche rescue took place at Montana's Big Sky ski resort. Bill Larch, owner of Gallatin Search Dogs, had instructed the volunteer to put his hands in front of his face to create a breathing space. Then he began piling snow on top of him. The volunteer described his "burial" experience:

> The first thing that struck me was the weight. . . . I opened my eyes and blinked a few times . . . my hole was so dark I thought for a few panicked seconds that I'd gone blind. . . . A chill started at the tips of my toes, and like a flash it washed over my body, producing a violent shivering that cramped my muscles. My fingers were the worst; even with gloves on, they became numb and functionless. . . . I begged for freedom. [Then] I heard . . . scratching . . . then . . . barking. There was a crack of light, the furry tip of a paw . . . blue, blue skies . . . a warm, wet lick across my face.[3]

This find of a live person does not always happen, however, in real avalanche searches. Survival statistics show 90

A black lab works with a ski patrolman to train for special certification as an avalanche rescue dog.

percent of avalanche victims are alive at the fifteen-minute mark. After thirty-five minutes, the survival rate is down to 30 percent.

Training and certification requirements are similar for all search-and-rescue teams, although some focus more on one type of training—such as avalanche or wilderness—for example. But their primary objective is rescuing people.

Chapter Three

Rescue Dogs on the Job

Search-and-rescue organizations may respond to as many as one hundred calls for help each year. Police and anxious relatives count on the dogs to do a job that otherwise would require many hours of work from dozens of searchers. One dog can do the work of twenty to thirty people.

The search-and-rescue teams are called to duty by public agencies such as police and fire departments or national park services. The units provide free services. They are all volunteers and receive no salary. However, donations of money, supplies, and equipment are provided by businesses, organizations, and people in the community.

Ready in a Jiffy

Handlers and rescue dogs must be packed and ready at all times because a quick response is essential to saving lives.

Hank Whittemore described a typical scenario at handler Caroline Hebards' home in Bernardsville, New Jersey:

> The phone rang in the dim light of the kitchen, where Aly lay half sleeping on the floor, and he heard the voice of his human partner answer it upstairs. He remained still for several minutes, but then a different noise reached his sensitive German shepherd ears, causing them to twitch and move forward. Now Aly listened intently to what, for him, was the most thrilling sound in the world:

A search-and-rescue team takes a few minutes to relax while waiting to be sent to a rescue site.

Caroline, up on the second floor, had swung open the door of her search-and-rescue closet, where all the gear was stowed. . . . When he heard her footsteps on the stairs and realized that she was wearing hiking boots, his movements quickened with excitement; seeing her familiar orange coverall, Aly produced a joyful bark to let her know he was ready. It was time to get to work.[4]

Some dogs wear a backpack of supplies that includes a headlamp for working in dark places, harness straps, first aid materials, dog cookies, and a canine energy drink. The first aid supplies are for both the victim and the dog. Other dogs wear a vest bearing a white cross and the word RESCUE on it. Dogs get excited when this uniform is put on them because they know they are going on a job assignment.

Dog Searchers Prove Their Efficiency

One such job assignment was given to Pativ, a German shepherd. A toddler, Erica Booth, had wandered away from her father's towing business in Lincoln, Massachusetts. Sixty-five searchers, using two thermal-imaging cameras, a helicopter, and floodlights, hunted in vain for Erica. Then Pativ was brought to the scene. Pativ quickly located the little girl. She had fallen asleep in a big cardboard box and was hidden by the box flaps. Pativ's excited barks woke her up—much to the relief of her parents and the searchers.

Children are not the only ones who get lost. Many others, including the elderly, may become missing. An el-

A dog uses its powerful sense of smell to sniff for people buried by earthquake debris.

derly person may stroll away from home or from a nursing facility. One eighty-eight-year-old woman walked out of a nursing home during a pounding rainstorm. Searchers had already spent eighteen hours looking for the woman before calling Marcia Koenig and her German shepherd Coyote.

> I gave Coyote a scent article and she found [the woman] within ten minutes. [The lost woman] was less than a quarter-mile from the home, but she was lying down, concealed in some bushes. I yelled "Good dog!" to Coyote, and then ran to the woman. Thank God, she was still alive.[5]

But not all searches end so happily.

A Water Rescue

When an eight-year-old boy wandered away from home and could not be found for two days, Caroline Hebard received a call from the police. She arrived with Aly on the third day of the search. The nearby woods and fields had been combed by hundreds of officers and volunteers.

Caroline and Aly began from where the boy was last seen. Aly picked up a scent pattern but did not seem too enthused. Then Aly led Caroline down to a riverbank. He walked along the edge, sniffing, and then barking. After obtaining a motorized rubber raft, the police took Caroline and Aly onto the river. In the middle of the river, Aly leaned overboard and barked. A police diver was sent down to search. He found the boy's body ten minutes later. It is not known how the boy's body ended up in the river.

Caroline and Aly also used their search-and-rescue skills in the 1985 Mexico City earthquake, in the 1986 San Salvador earthquake, in the 1988 Armenian earthquake, and in 1989 in South Carolina during Hurricane Hugo.

Transportation to Disaster Sites

When dog teams are flown to international disaster areas, they usually fly in huge military cargo planes, which are like large warehouses inside. The cargo plane's entire rear end opens up for loading supplies. The handlers sit on benches with their dogs.

Oklahoma City Disaster

Sometimes a situation requires more than one search dog. In large disasters, for example, there may be several dogs trained in different specialties. Some locate bombs; others find live people; and still others sniff for corpses.

On April 19, 1995, an explosion ripped through the Alfred P. Murrah Federal Building in Oklahoma City, Oklahoma. The building collapsed, killing nearly 170 people and trapping hundreds of others.

Some dogs are trained to sniff out bombs as this dog shows in a training exercise.

The first dog on the scene was Bennie, a bomb-seeking German shepherd. Bennie's job was to sniff the air and the ground to make sure there were no more explosions. This provided some assurance that the area was safe for human rescue workers.

Next, Bronte, a rottweiler, went to work. In some emergencies, rescue dogs are trained to find live victims and ignore dead bodies. During Bronte's first twenty-minute shift, she alerted her handler, Steve Powell, to the same place four times. "But it was only a halfway alert. She didn't bark. I didn't know what to make of it. I looked at that pile of rubble, and I didn't see how anyone could survive under there."[6]

Excavators came to the spot anyway and began digging. Three hours later they lifted out fifteen-year-old Brandi Liggons, still alive. Bronte had been puzzled because the girl was pinned beside her friend—who had died.

Emotional Stress Takes Its Toll

In the disaster, dozens of team handlers were credited with leading emergency crews to the bodies of at least fifty victims. Few dogs that worked the Oklahoma site sustained any physical injuries. Neither did the handlers. But the handlers suffered emotionally, and the stress of such work takes its toll. According to a survey, sixteen teams left search-and-rescue work due to the **emotional** impact of that event.

Disasters affect humans more than dogs. After dealing with a flood disaster, Caroline Hebard said, "Search-and-rescue work was often rewarding but seldom if ever

A busy rescue site, such as the federal building in Oklahoma City (pictured here), can cause emotional stress for dogs and their handlers.

glamorous. It was usually filthy and exhausting. It could expose a person to devastation and death and engrave images of suffering on the mind and soul."[7]

Nevertheless, many dogs and their handlers continue performing their courageous feats. And along the way, they discover even more daring ways to do so.

New Breakthroughs

In 1994 a Newfoundland named Mas was the first to leap from a helicopter that was hovering at twelve feet above the water. A drowning person can grab onto the huge dog's fur or the dog can bring the victim a lifeline from

Whether rescues take place in water, rubble, or on snowy peaks, emotional stress takes its toll on everyone involved.

the helicopter. Such daring rescues offer crews much greater flexibility with response time. For example, helicopters can fly to drowning victims faster than boats or swimming dogs can get there, especially if the accident is far from shore.

Now other Newfoundland dogs are being schooled for helicopter rescues. Before Mas made his first jump from a helicopter, he had been trained to perform progressively difficult aquatic feats: diving off piers; rescuing a person in the breakers; swimming a mile to a drowning victim to pull the person to safety; and towing a boat.

Rescue teams accept the strenuous toil of their jobs, but they also enjoy training activities when they are off duty.

Chapter Four

Off-Duty Activities

After a disaster or other type of rescue job, a dog and its handler return home to wait for the next assignment. During this waiting time, the dog is the family pet. But to stay sharp, the dog and its handler also continue their practice sessions.

Strain on the Handler's Family Life

Many volunteer handlers drop out of the program once they realize that training and maintaining the skills of both themselves and their dogs can require as many as one thousand hours of work a year. During training and at work, the job of a rescue dog is strenuous, both mentally and physically. The dogs must practice commands. They also must walk long distances, climb through debris, swim, and dig through snow. The work is also demanding for handlers.

Caroline Hebard tells a search coleader how she runs her rescue responsibilities and the household at the same time:

A handler and her rescue dog rest for a moment amidst the wreckage of a collapsed building.

[My husband] and the kids are totally supportive. They accept what I do and I think they're proud of me, but I know that my rescue work often disrupts their lives. When I come back from a search, they don't want to hear about what I've seen and done. What they want is to get their routines back on track.

So I have to block out what I just went through and fall back into the role of mom. I've learned to keep the other side of my life away from them. I think, **psychologically** [emotionally], they feel safer not knowing about any of the risks I take. And I never force it on them.[8]

Requirements for Handlers

Handlers, as well as dogs, must maintain skills between rescue jobs. First, they must stay in top physical condition. The variety of training exercises for handlers includes backpacking over difficult terrain, wilderness survival, and cross-country skiing. A handler also descends steep cliffs with his or her ninety-pound dog harnessed to the same line. In addition, handlers need skills in first aid, map reading, and compass reading. Handlers pay for their own food, travel, equipment, and training, which can amount to as much as $8,000 per year.

Support Organizations

No matter what their specialty, dog/handler teams usually join an organization that helps with training and testing. Approximately one hundred rescue teams are members of the American Rescue Dog Association (ARDA). Founded

A volunteer checks a rescue dog's paws for injuries after searching through the rubble at the World Trade Center site.

in 1972, ARDA is the nation's oldest air-scenting search dog organization. Their standards and training methods have served as the model for dog/handler teams.

In the United States, many private rescue teams are made up of volunteers. The volunteers come from all walks of life, and in the United States, 65 percent are female. In addition, more than 150 groups of search-and-rescue organizations service the country.

Handler Judgment

Handlers also must make decisions regarding the health of their dogs. They must decide when to take the dog out of rescue work. Some dogs will work until the age of eight or nine before they retire. Some go off duty at a younger age.

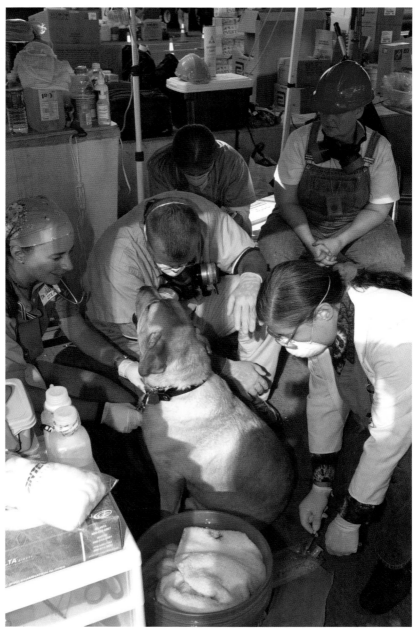

This rescue dog receives medical treatment from a specially trained canine team. Many disaster sites have first aid stations set up for both people and dogs.

Big dogs, such as German shepherds, are susceptible to a disabling condition called hip dysplasia. It may at first look like a wobbly walk. It may even happen at a young age. If that happens, the dog cannot be bred, nor can it be a working dog, because it will not be able to perform strenuous tasks required for search and rescue. This dog will then be kept as a family pet or adopted by others. Many people are on a waiting list to adopt these valuable dogs.

Euthanasia Decisions

Like any pet owner, handlers are extremely saddened if their once-healthy dogs contract a **terminal** illness. These situations may require the handler to have his or her partner put to sleep. Caroline Hebard shares such an experience involving Zibo, her beloved eight-year-old German shepherd.

One morning she unexpectedly found Zibo unable to move in his pen. Zibo just laid there. He could not move his hind legs or tail or even bark. The night before, Zibo had been his normally, bouncy, energetic self—playing with Caroline's puppy, Sasquatch.

Caroline explained to her children that Zibo had had a massive stroke and that she would have to put Zibo down. At the vet's office, Caroline held Zibo's head in her lap as the vet gave the dog a **lethal** injection. Caroline watched as her partner drifted into sleep.

After Zibo died, Sasquatch mourned the loss of his buddy and stopped eating for a while. To comfort himself, during a month-long mourning period, Sasquatch

A rescue dog is honored for its work at the site of the Oklahoma City federal building bombing.

slept with an old broom with bristles that resembled Zibo's wiry, coarse hair.

Rescue Dog Drop-Out

Sasquatch was Caroline Hebard's next partner. During that time, she had begun to host wilderness-survival programs. Caroline taught classes to local students and adults on how to prevent getting lost in the woods and what to do if they did. Sasquatch was part of the program. However, Sasquatch became a master clown on the stage, rolling on his back, paws waving in the air, and distracting Caroline's giggling audience.

Sasquatch also displayed a limited attention span in the field. He loved chasing rabbits, squirrels, and deer. On one search, Sasquatch cornered a wild turkey; on another he raced onto a farm and sent all the chickens flapping into trees. Despite her skillful training methods, Caroline finally had to admit that Sasquatch did not have the personality of a rescue dog. He was too easily distracted. Consequently, Sasquatch had to be retired from the program. He became their family dog and lived for thirteen years.

However, for those dogs with the right characteristics and desires, a special job is waiting for them. These dogs are valuable assets in search-and-rescue jobs. On any given day, the dogs are ready to find and rescue lost people. They perform well in forbidding wilderness, deep snow, icy water, and at major disaster scenes. And they outperform humans both with the endurance and energy required to save lives.

Notes

Chapter One: The Job of Rescue Dogs

1. Quoted in Jared Sandberg "Porkchop Is Among Hero Dogs Combing Trade Center Rubble—Trained to Sniff Out the Living and the Dead, Hundreds Gladly Work 12-Hour Shifts," *Wall Street Journal,* September 25, 2001, p. A 1.

Chapter Two: Training

2. Quoted in Rebecca Sweat, "Hero Hounds That Sniff Out and Rescue People," PetPlace.com.

3. Quoted in "Six Feet Under," *Skiing,* October 1993, p. 28.

Chapter Three: Rescue Dogs on the Job

4. Hank Whittemore and Caroline Hebard, *So That Others May Live.* New York: Bantam Books, 1995, pp. 1–2.

5. Quoted in Catherine Dold, "For Rescue Dogs 'Nothing's Better than a Live Find,'" *Smithsonian,* August 1997, p. 79.

6. Quoted in Suzanne Emler, "Dogs to the Rescue," *Boys' Life,* October 1997, p. 54.

7. Whittemore and Hebard, *So That Others May Live,* p. 70.

Chapter Four: Off-Duty Activities

8. Quoted in Whittemore and Hebard, *So That Others May Live,* pp. 192–93.

Glossary

agility: The ability to make quick and easy movements.

avalanches: A large amount of snow or rock that suddenly slides down a mountain.

corpse: A dead body.

deployed: Rescue teams sent out to a specific area.

earthquakes: A series of vibrations in the earth's crust causing land movement.

emotional: Pertaining to feelings of emotions such as joy, sorrow, or hate.

lethal: Causing death.

placenta: An organ that partially surrounds the fetus in female mammals during pregnancy.

psychologically: Of the mind.

suffocate: To die from lack of oxygen.

terminal: The last illness or a deadly illness.

Organizations to Contact

The American Rescue Dog Association (ARDA), New Jersey
Penny Sullivan
PO Box 151
Chester, NY 10918
(845) 469-4173
www.ardainc.org
Founded in 1972, ARDA is the nation's oldest air-scenting search-dog organization. Its training methods are the model for dog teams around the nation.

National Association for Search and Rescue (NASAR)
4500 Southgate Pl., Suite 100
Chantilly, VA 20151-1714
(703) 222-6277
www.nasar.org
NASAR has a membership of thousands of dedicated paid workers and unpaid volunteers committed to the cause of saving lives.

National Disaster Search Dog Foundation
PMB #245
323 E. Matilija, Suite 110
Ojai, CA 93023-2740

(888) 646-1242

www.ndsdf.org

The foundation's mission is to provide highly trained dogs to search for live victims. This site includes frequently asked questions.

WOOF Search Dogs

Marin County Sheriff's Department

Civic Center

San Rafael, CA 94903

(415) 499-7243

www.searchdogs.com

The Wilderness Finders, Inc. (WOOF) is on call twenty-four hours a day to the entire United States, with most calls coming from California and Nevada.

For Further Exploration

Books

Charles and Linda George, *Search and Rescue Dogs.* New York: Franklin Watts, 1998. Describes the history, selection, training, and accomplishments of different dogs used in search-and-rescue operations.

Elizabeth Ring, *Search and Rescue Dogs.* Brookfield, CT: Millbrook Press, 1994. Dogs of all breeds (including mixed breeds) can be trained as search-and-rescue dogs. This book describes these nose-to-the-ground rescue workers and the organizations that direct their work.

Charlotte Wilcox, *The Newfoundland.* Mankato, MN: Capstone High/Low Books, 1999. Introduces the history, development, uses, and care of this dog breed, known for life-saving and search-and-rescue work.

Periodical

Kristin Baird Rattini, "Dogs to the Rescue," *National Geographic World,* December 2001. Canine heroes put their best paw forward in New York City and Washington, D.C., after the September 11, 2001, terrorist attacks.

Index

Picture Credits

About the Author

Judith Janda Presnall is an award-winning nonfiction writer. Her books include *Rachel Carson, Artificial Organs, The Giant Panda, Oprah Winfrey, Mount Rushmore, Life on Alcatraz, Animals That Glow, Animal Skeletons,* and *Circuses.* Presnall graduated from the University of Wisconsin in Whitewater. She is a recipient of the Jack London Award for meritorious service in the California Writers Club. She is also a member of the Society of Children's Book Writers and Illustrators. Judith lives in the Los Angeles area with her husband Lance and three cats.